To Gabriell

Love
♡

Great Grandma &
Great Grandpa Gilbert

A Picture Book of

FARM ANIMALS

Written by Mary Scott
Illustrated by Lisa C. Botto

Troll Associates

Library of Congress Cataloging-in-Publication Data

Scott, Mary, (date)
  A picture book of farm animals / by Mary Scott; illustrated by
Lisa C. Botto.
    p.   cm.
  Summary: Examines a variety of farm animals, including cattle,
sheep, hogs, and ducks.
  ISBN 0-8167-2150-5 (lib. bdg.)   ISBN 0-8167-2151-3 (pbk.)
  1. Domestic animals—Juvenile literature.   [1. Domestic animals.]
I. Botto, Lisa C., 1965-   ill.   II. Title.
SF75.5.S37   1991
636-dc20   90-44888

Printed in the United States of America.
10 9 8 7 6 5 4 3 2

Many different animals live on a farm.
The horses live in the stable.
The cows are in the field.
The chickens are in the barnyard.

What other
animals live
on a farm?

CATTLE

Cattle are important farm animals. Some farmers raise cattle for meat and milk. In some parts of the world, farmers use cattle to pull plows and wagons.

Male cattle are called *bulls*. Females are *cows*, and young cattle are *calves*. The cattle in this picture are *dairy cows*. They give us milk.

HORSE

Many years ago, horses were important farm animals. Before people had trucks and other machines, farmers used horses to pull plows and do other work. Today, most farm horses are ridden for fun.

A horse's body helps it run for long periods of time. Its legs are long and strong, so it can run quickly. It has wide nostrils and large, powerful lungs to help it breathe easily. A horse is also smart enough to learn many commands.

GOAT

Like cows, goats are often raised on farms for their milk. Goats are also covered with wool fleece, like sheep.

Female *nanny* goats and male *billy* goats have horns. Young goats are called *kids.* Goats eat corn, oats, grass, and other plants. They've also been known to eat hats and paper, too!

HOG

Hogs, or pigs as they are usually called, are very smart farm animals. You may think hogs are dirty because they like to roll around in mud. However, hogs are not being messy—they are just trying to keep cool. Under all that mud, hogs can be many colors, such as pink, or black, or even white.

DUCK

Ducks are very lively farm animals. They like to swim in ponds and play with the other small animals in the barnyard. Ducks usually travel in groups, called a *flock*. These are *White Pekins*, the most common ducks raised on farms.

Ducklings, or baby ducks, are covered with soft fluff called *down.* Ducklings can run, swim, and find food soon after they are born. But they can't fly until they are 5-8 weeks old! By then, they have feathers and look just like their mother and father.

GOOSE

There are many different kinds of geese.

These are wild *Canada geese*. They do not live on the farm. They are often found living in ponds and lakes.

A goose's wings and tail are covered with stiff *flight feathers*. They help the goose fly long distances. Underneath its feathers, a goose has a thick coat of *down*. These soft, white feathers keep the goose warm.

Down keeps people warm, too. Some farmers sell goose down to make soft, warm stuffing for sleeping bags and coats.

barnyard geese

Canada goose

RABBIT

Many people like to keep rabbits as pets. But while pet rabbits are fun to keep, wild rabbits can do a lot of damage to a farm. They love to eat all the plants that grow in the farmer's garden.

Rabbits don't walk on four legs like other animals do. They hop. By using their long back legs and short front legs, a rabbit can hop up to 10 feet in one jump!

CAT

Most people know that cats make excellent house pets. But did you know that cats are great hunters, too? A cat's muscles are long and thin, so it can move quickly. It can also jump easily, and it can turn its head to reach almost every part of its body.

On a farm, cats prowl around barns and storage areas, looking for mice.

Mice like to eat grain and other food the farmer needs for his cattle and horses. When a mouse is caught, the cat is the farmer's best helper.

DOG

Almost every farm has at least one dog. Dogs are very helpful farm animals. Some dogs help farmers by *herding* cattle or sheep. They protect the animals from wolves and other enemies, and make sure the animals do not wander away. Other dogs chase the wild rabbits away so they won't eat the farmer's vegetables.

Some farm dogs are kept only as family pets. It's nice to relax with a pet dog after a hard day's work on the farm.

DONKEY

Donkeys look a lot like small horses. That is because donkeys and horses are part of the same family. Some donkeys are small and fast. They are good for riding. Other donkeys are larger and slower. They can pull wagons or carry heavy loads on their backs.

Like most farm animals, donkeys can make good pets, but only if they are treated well. A donkey can become stubborn and mean if it is not treated with care.

CHICKEN

A chicken is a special kind of bird that gives us meat and eggs to eat. Like cattle, chickens are very important farm animals. Long ago, chickens were kept on farms to help feed the farmer's family. Today, most chickens are raised on very large farms. Some of these farms have millions of chickens!

The male chicken is called a *rooster*. It has a bright red *comb* on the top of its head and red *wattles* hanging down from its beak. Female chickens, called *hens*, lay many eggs each day. Some of these eggs are special—they have tiny baby *chicks* inside them! Farmers do not bring these eggs to the market.

SHEEP

These baby sheep, called *lambs*, are eating with their mother. Sheep like to eat grass and other plants that grow in the pasture. Some farmers keep small groups of sheep in fenced-in pastures. Others raise thousands of sheep on many acres of land.

In the winter, sheep are covered with a heavy coat of wool called *fleece*.

TURKEY

Turkeys and chickens are part of the same bird family. But turkeys are bigger than chickens. Male turkeys are called *toms*. Females are *hens*, and baby turkeys are *poults*. Like all farm animals, turkeys are very important for farmers, their families, and you, too.

Perhaps one day you will visit a farm and see all the special animals there. You can see the turkeys and chickens and pet the baby lambs. Maybe you can even ride on a horse! Farms are so much fun!